Welfare after Communism

János Kornai is Allie S. Freed Professor of Economics, Harvard University and Permanent Fellow, Collegium Budapest, Institute for Advanced Study. His book *From Socialism to Capitalism* was published by the Centre for Post-Collectivist Studies in 1997.

THE CENTRE FOR POST-COLLECTIVIST STUDIES

The Centre for Post-Collectivist Studies was set up in 1995 as an autonomous group within the Social Market Foundation. Its main activity is to study the global move towards market economy with a social market framework.

The Foundation's main activity is to commission and publish original papers by independent academic and other experts on key topics in the economic and social fields, with a view to stimulating public discussion on the performance of markets and the social framework within which they operate.

The Foundation is a registered charity and a company limited by guarantee. It is independent of any political party or group and is financed by the sales of publications and by voluntary donations from individuals, organisations and companies.

The views expressed in publications are those of the authors and do not represent a corporate opinion of the Foundation.

Welfare after Communism

JÁNOS KORNAI

The Social Market Foundation
Centre for Post-Collectivist Studies
December 1999

First published by The Social Market Foundation, 1999

The Social Market Foundation
11 Tufton Street
London SW1P 3QB

ISBN 1 874097 38 0

Contents

Acknowledgements	
Foreword	i
1. The State of the Welfare Sector	1
2. The Object of this Paper	5
3. The Ethical Dimension	8
4. Desired Features of Reformed Institutions	14
5. Desired Proportions of Allocation	28
6. Conclusion	34
References	38
Notes	42
SMF Publications	

Acknowledgements

This paper draws extensively on Kornai (1997). I am grateful to Daniel Bell, Zsuzsa Dániel, Peter Diamond, Robert Dorfman, Robert Iván Gál, Mária Kovács, Amartya Sen, András Simonovits and István György Tóth. I express my gratitude to Ágnes Benedict, Béla Janky and Virág Molnár for their helpful research assistance, to Brian McLean for his excellent translation of the text and to Julianna Parti for her assistance in editing this paper. The research was supported by the Hungarian National Scientific Research Foundation (OTKA 018280).

Foreword

Reform of the welfare states of the post-communist countries has so far been the poor relation of economic reform. Interestingly, this has not been due to any fundamental difference in the state of disarray of the economic and welfare systems. The deposed communist governments of the former Soviet Union and Eastern Europe bequeathed their successors crumbling and state-monopolised economies and welfare systems in a near identical state. The ongoing transition from communism to capitalism has had similar effects on both the welfare and productive sectors in most post-communist countries. As production fell in the post-communist economies, the real value of pensions and other government transfers plummeted. Despite these similarities, the state of reforms in these sectors could not be more different.

The reform of economic, legal and political institutions has been widespread and has generated enthusiasm amongst Western countries, international financial and aid organisations as well as the new generations of politicians in the transition countries. However, this activity and interest has not been matched in the welfare sector of transition economies. While the state monopoly of production has been reduced, and increased freedom and choice has been introduced into the economies of the post-collectivist countries, the state monopoly in welfare provision has been left untouched and choice has little role in the welfare sector. As this paper shows, welfare reform also lacks the first principles that the ideal of the free market affords economic reform, and the historical failure for Western nations to create effective, efficient and affordable welfare states robs reformers of role models in the West that are available in the economic and political sphere.

Professor Kornai's admirable book seeks to change this imbalance of interest and activity, and to provide explicit first principles that can play the role for welfare reform that the competitive market has played for economic reform. Kornai recognises the *ad hoc* nature of the debates on reform of the welfare sector and formulates a set of nine internally consistent principles that inform his ideas about the future for welfare systems in the former communist countries. The author carves out a new agenda for reform based on principles that 'have both feet planted in capitalism' but at the same time seek to avoid what Kenneth Arrow has deemed 'worship of the market'. In doing so Kornai hopes to marry the efficiency of decentralised incentives and decision making to a concern for social welfare and cohesion. It is in presenting this new agenda that this book adds most to the fractured and polarised debates on the welfare state - both in the transition countries and in the West.

That Kornai succeeds in his aims of providing a clear philosophical basis for the reform of the state-monopolised welfare system seems clear. What remains to be seen is how quickly and with how much vigour the people of the transition countries and the developed world, and their political representatives, respond to his ideas. In the current intellectual market that often seems, quite frankly, starved of coherent and clear agendas for welfare reform, it may be quite quickly and with the same sort of vigour that was first shown in the reform of the command economies. If reformers take up Kornai's challenge and accept that welfare reform cannot be a 'quick fix', perhaps the reform of the welfare state will not only begin in earnest but avoid many of the problems of economic reform that still hamper the enormous potential of Eastern Europe.

Donald McCarthy
Centre for Post-Collectivist Studies
1999

1. The State of the Welfare Sector

All over the world, efforts have begun to reform the welfare sector, or at least to debate how it should be changed.

What do I mean by the welfare sector? I refrain here from defining it as a concept. Let me describe it by listing its main components: the pension system, health care, provision for children, the sick and the aged outside the home, and allowances awarded on various grounds. There are also activities and institutions that some would include in the concept of the welfare sector and some omit: public education, state subsidies on goods and services supplying basic needs, social housing, and so on. My interpretation of the welfare sector is certainly broad and comprehensive, so that it can be divided into several sub-sectors accommodating the majority of those areas which have generally until now been seen as public sector responsibilities. But I should warn that this study does not deal with welfare problems related to unemployment.[1]

The 'welfare state' undertakes to control and/or finance many parts of the welfare sector. The debate concerns, among other questions, which of the activities and institutions generally perceived as belonging to the welfare sector should fall within the competence of the state.

The process of change has proved difficult everywhere. In the United States, the Clinton administration's health care reform was a political failure, and the conservatives' efforts to bring about a radical cut in welfare spending broke down amid bad political reactions. In Germany and Austria, there arose strong resistance, in and outside the legislature, to quite modest reductions of a few percentage points in the budget's welfare spending. A similar attempt in France caused a strike that lasted several weeks, crippling the capital.

If the process seems difficult in rich, developed countries, what can be expected in the post-socialist countries, where the conditions for reform are far less favourable? The welfare sectors of the socialist countries differed in many respects, but they shared several features that left their mark on the legacy bequeathed after the change of system.

The state in the Soviet Union and the East European socialist countries had made legal commitments to provide universal welfare services.[2] The entitlements applied to every citizen, or to every employee, which, with full employment, more or less coincided with rights for every citizen. The state's commitments included free health care and free education, including higher education, and a state pension for every worker. Furthermore, there were high state subsidies on articles covering basic needs (such as food and housing), a system of almost free day-nurseries, kindergartens and after-school centres, and many other state welfare services. Non-state provision of welfare services was not permitted.

The public had ambivalent feelings about the condition of the welfare sector. People almost took for granted the state's extreme paternalism and their consequent material security, for the care included a virtual guarantee that everyone's basic needs would be met. On the other hand, people felt that the standard of many welfare services was low. Medical care might be free, but hospital equipment and medical supplies were poor. Housing might be cheap and homelessness non-existent, but the living space averaged out at only a couple of square metres per head. Many people were reduced to living in crowded workers' hostels or multi-occupied 'communal' flats, and many of the buildings were in run-down condition. Every worker might be entitled to a state pension, but the provision left many pensioners subsisting in poverty. The universal entitlements aroused great expectations in the public, who felt that the socialist state had failed to keep its promises and guarantee them real welfare.

What effects did the dramatic changes of 1989–91 bring to the welfare sector? There are great differences between the countries of the region, but it is worthwhile to emphasise certain important common features of their development in the last few years. The post-socialist countries experienced the deepest economic crises in their history. Production fell drastically, along with household income and consumption. There was a painful drop in the purchasing power of the already very modest monetary transfers (pensions, allowances and so on). The standard of services in kind (such as health care) deteriorated further for lack of adequate funding. Broad segments of the population in many countries sank below the poverty line of minimum subsistence. Many post-socialist economies, already suffering from serious fiscal deficits, plunged, or were clearly about to plunge, into fiscal crisis. This meant they became unable to ensure even a minimal fulfilment of the state's universal commitments.

In post-socialist societies the sense of security, hitherto seemingly self-evident, was shaken. Full employment and even labour shortage abruptly gave way to mass, persistent unemployment. Debate about reforming the welfare state began. The public faced the prospect of losing previous entitlements, whereas most people had hoped for the opposite with the change in regime. They had expected the pledge enshrined in the law, which the socialist system had kept, but to a disappointingly low standard, to be redeemed under the new system at a much higher level. This gulf between the state's commitments, the expectations engendered by them and their actual fulfilment caused perpetual tension.

Great strides have been made in the post-socialist region with transforming political and economic institutions and the legal system. Reform of the welfare sector is the sphere of transformation where the least progress has occurred. Indeed there has hardly been any change at all. While the role of the state in other social and economic spheres has been narrowed or transformed considerably, in the welfare sector it has remained almost as bloated as before, leaving insufficient scope for private enterprise or for freedom of choice. The socialist system with all its well-known features has survived in the welfare sector. There is an almost total monopoly of state ownership, the legal private sector is very small and restricted by various bureaucratic and economic constraints. A command economy applies, with strong centralisation, 'rationing' and bureaucratic coordination. Only traces of the market mechanism can be observed. Market prices hardly play any part at all. The chronic shortage economy that prevails here shows the usual symptoms: forced substitution, queuing and waiting, and personal connections and corruption to side-step the bureaucratic procedures. The bureaucracy that runs the state and semi-state, corporatist welfare sector, fearing erosion of its power, resists all reforms that point towards decentralisation, competition and the market.

Reform proves hard not just because it has sensitive effects on people's lives. It is easy to be blown off course, for want of a compass. When it came to establishing a stock market, the experience of the New York, Zurich or Frankfurt stock exchanges was available. When the statutes for a central bank compatible with a market economy were being drafted, the Bank of England, the Federal Reserve and the Bundesbank could offer patterns. Much the same can be said of problems like the competence of the supreme court or the rules of corporate governance. But who is going to teach the post-socialist countries how to run an efficient welfare state? No country can really serve as an example. Every welfare state without exception, in the most developed or medium-income countries alike, operates dysfunctionally, and faces a present or future crisis. The post-socialist countries will have to undertake for themselves the design of the kind of welfare sector they need.

2. The Object of this Paper

The debates are in chaos. They take place on various planes: among politicians, within and between political parties, between finance ministry bureaucrats and those of ministries controlling and supervising the welfare sector, among opposing pressure groups, and among various schools of thought in the academic world. It is very hard for those who set about devising reform proposals to find their way through this labyrinth.

This partly explains how the practical plans of reform come to lack a basis in principle. Sometimes the philosophy behind a plan can be picked out. Other schemes reflect a bewildered compromise between diametrically opposing principles, or have not been thought out at all.

This study seeks to contribute to *clarifying the principles* on which reform of the welfare sector should rest. It does not describe positive research into the present state of affairs. It aims at an exclusively normative approach to the problem.

The various post-socialist countries differ in the present state of their welfare sectors and in the conditions for implementing reforms. Nonetheless, the starting points show enough common features to allow the formulation of some common principles, applicable to all post-socialist countries. Even if those applying the reforms agreed on the principles to be expounded here, countries would still differ, of course, on many details of implementation, on the pace of the process, and on the means to be used.

This paper sets out nine principles.[3] I accept that they are not all of equal weight, but to avoid confusion I do not propose to sub-divide them into principles, rules, guidelines etc., because they are designed to work together and reinforce one another within a specific hierarchical structure. Chapter Three is devoted to principles 1 and 2, which state the basic or primary values to be applied. They are the fundamental ethical postulates, providing the background guidance for the formulation of the institutional and micro-economic principles numbered 3 to 7, presented in Chapter Four; and for the macro-economic principles 8 and 9, contained in Chapter Five, which are required to deliver the allocation proportions desirable for the welfare sector.

For the sake of convenience and ready reference, the principles are listed below:

Principle 1: Sovereignty of the individual
Principle 2: Solidarity
Principle 3: Competition
Principle 4: Incentives
Principle 5: A new role for the state
Principle 6: Transparency
Principle 7: The time requirement of the programme
Principle 8: Harmonious growth
Principle 9: Sustainable financing

Ideally, it would have been better to conduct a far more rigorous, axiomatic discussion, starting from postulates and auxiliary postulates and conclusions drawn from them. That would have revealed that the principles are not just listed one after the other, but bear certain logical relations to each other, forming a closed theoretical structure. Unfortunately, this cannot be undertaken within the scope of a short paper - whose main purpose is to inject fresh thinking into the debate. Therefore, a lower level of abstraction is applied. I hope, however, that even this 'medium level' of abstraction and semi-exact mode of discussion will pay an intellectual premium over the usual lowly level of reform proposals. Perhaps it can at least help to transfer the debate from the details of some proposal or other to matters of principle. The medium level of generalisation seems sufficient for one of the study's objectives, which is to supply common principles on which to rest the otherwise separately treated parts of the reform: pension reform, health reform, allowances reform, and so on. Not least for reasons of space, the study cannot set forth practical proposals for the details of these reforms. There are only a few references to such proposals, simply to illustrate the principles.[4]

The study adopts the imperative mood to express the principles. The calls are addressed to the 'reformer'. This may be a politician, an official, an expert adviser, a union official, or an academic. Each principle is a *memento* — something to keep in mind when proposing a reform. It reveals also a *credo*, espousing my own set of values underlying my proposals. Since the principles to be expounded rest on my chosen system of values, and to that extent are subjective, I feel justified, at several places in this study, in presenting my message expressly in the first person singular.

3. The Ethical Dimension

Although I am an economist, I do not start out from economic principles. I am not one of those who advocate reform of the welfare sector mainly because its costs cannot be financed, and will be even less possible to finance in the future. Mention will be made later of economic principles as well, but I do not consider them as the fundament for the reform.

Here I put forward two ethical principles that I consider reformers should follow.[5] The institutions and allocation proportions that develop during the reform must be in line with these moral imperatives.

Principle 1 (sovereignty of the individual): The transformation promoted must increase the scope for the individual and reduce the scope for the state to decide in the sphere of welfare services.

The main trouble with the welfare system inherited from the socialist system, I consider, is that it leaves too wide a range of resources in the hands of the government, the political process and the bureaucracy, instead of the individual. This infringes on such fundamental human rights as individual sovereignty, self-realisation and self-determination.[6] When the welfare spending of the budget decreases, along with the taxes to finance it, citizens are not just having rights withdrawn; more pertinently, they are regaining rights of individual disposal.

Principle 1 includes not only the individual's decision-making rights, but the requirement that individuals be *responsible* for their own lives. They must give up the habit of allowing the paternalist state to think for them (and be helped by the reformers in this detoxification cure). After that, they have far more of a right to choose, but they are also responsible for their choices, bearing the consequences if their decisions are bad. In the Western world this is considered a trivial requirement, imbibed by all citizens with their mother's milk. However, for generations that grew up under the socialist system the opposite was instilled: the idea that the ruling party and the state are responsible for everything, and individuals should accept their decisions, feeling they are in good hands. So when people have a problem, their first thought is not to solve it for themselves, but to call for help from the state. The state will be at hand, so that they have no need to prepare for the uncertainties of the morrow.[7] The reform of the welfare state is based on the development of a new ethos that brings the sovereignty and responsibility of the individual to the fore.

It also follows from Principle 1 that although no actual society can function without some governmental coercion, it is desirable to minimise this, and place in the forefront the principle of *voluntary action*. Paternalism tries to impose 'forced happiness' on people. Instead, people should be allowed to pursue happiness for themselves.

Principle 2 (solidarity): Help the suffering, the troubled and the disadvantaged.

Many religions, including Judeo-Christian and Buddhist ethics, urge compassionate solidarity, as do labour movement traditions and left-wing political beliefs. The same sentiments may arise out of plain human goodwill, a sense of fraternity and community, and an innate altruistic sensibility, without necessarily being based on any specific world view or intellectual tradition.

The solidarity principle suggests that, apart from individual and collective charitable work, the community should help the suffering, troubled and disadvantaged through a system of *state* redistribution. Let us not explore here the criteria for receiving *state* assistance. Suffice it to say, that the set of those in need of communal aid will be much narrower than the community as a whole.[8]

Implementation of the solidarity principle requires *targeted* state assistance, not universal entitlements — state benefits awarded as a citizen's right to everyone, rich and poor, needy and self-sufficient. Principle 2 *does not exclude* the possibility of legislating universal state commitments, but it does not require them. Making commitments to give entitlements to all citizens and all employees conflicts with economic realities not moral imperatives. More will be said about this later, under Principles 8 and 9.

Principle 2 conflicts with the interest of politicians in turning the middle class into the main beneficiary of tax policy and redistribution. The middle class, by definition, is not in the greatest need of assistance. Under the socialist system, much of the redistributive process takes place within the middle class. The same applies to some extent in all countries where universal entitlements have developed strongly. The truly needy have never risen into the middle class, or have sunk beneath it.[9] These are the people whose assistance is preferred under Principle 2.

Behind the idea of Principle 2 lies the fundamental demand that every member of a community should be capable at least of satisfying his or her basic needs.[10] However, this does not imply that the state has to make the basic provisions free, or in the form of a preferential benefit, for *everyone*. Most members of society are capable of obtaining these by their own efforts. The principle of solidarity has to apply only to those who are incapable of supplying even their basic needs by their own efforts.

In the light of Principle 2, it is worth considering the issue of uncertainty about the future. Although one may not be dependent on anyone at present, one may *become* dependent in the future. But according to Principle 1, the individual must primarily prepare for such contingencies, by saving and building up reserves, and by voluntarily purchasing a private insurance policy of a commercial nature. The individual should be entitled to state assistance on a solidarity basis only if he encounters problems for which he could not have prepared by the individual means just mentioned.[11]

Principle 2 includes solidarity between generations, with a fair intergenerational distribution of life's cares and joys. The present generation has to show solidarity with future generations. There is no moral law that justifies making life easier today by leaving future generations grave debts, economic time-bombs exploding in the more distant future.[12]

Principle 2 requires that every citizen must be given a chance of successful self fulfilment. This is one of several arguments in favour of state support for public education.[13] Solidarity must be shown with those who will not receive this initial opportunity without state assistance. The criterion of solidarity can also justify 'affirmative action', i.e. active assistance to the disadvantaged, so as to ensure their initial opportunity. On the other hand, it cannot justify any kind of crude, artificial attempt to level the great differences between people.

Principle 2 must apply in conjunction with Principle 1. Most people find 'alms' demeaning. The needy must be helped primarily by giving them a chance to work and undertake useful activity. The extent to which claimants are capable of helping themselves and adapting to the situation must be considered when the degree and type of help is determined.

Principles 1 and 2 must also be considered together when a position is taken on *compulsory minimum insurance.* I support the idea of legally obliging all citizens to purchase minimum pension and health insurance. These policies could be held with decentralised insurance institutions. This restricts the application of Principle 1, because voluntary action gives way to a legal requirement. However, it does not have a paternalist intent. It is not an attempt to impose 'forced happiness' on people. The motive here is collective self-interest, not altruism. We know that a humane society will feel compelled to care for the sick who are bereft of treatment or the elderly who are left without income. They will be supported eventually at the taxpayers' expense. So it is to avoid this undesirable external effect that the law should oblige all citizens to obtain at least minimum insurance coverage.[14] Principle 2 — solidarity, society's collective altruism — steps in to help those not capable of paying the compulsory insurance. The difference between the proposed and the present schemes is conspicuous. There is either (i) minimum compulsory insurance, with voluntary insurance above the minimum and help for the needy by redistributive means, or (ii) universal entitlement, with the whole task of insurance channelled through paternalist state redistribution. The first seems to me a healthier, more efficient compromise between Principles 1 and 2.

One more comment seems apposite, to conclude the discussion on the ethical starting points. The line of argument in this study does not start from the *ultimate* values of freedom, equality, well-being and material welfare, or social justice. The relationships between ultimate values and social organisation are the concern of studies in political theory dealing with the ethical foundations of a 'good' society.[15] This paper does not set out to contribute to the analysis of these deeper problems. I hope that Principles 1 and 2, which identify 'intermediate' ethical requirements, not ultimate values, can provide a broad platform, acceptable to people who take differing views on freedom, equality and social justice.

On the other hand, Principle 1 will be alien (and Principle 2 may be superfluous) to those whose axiomatic point of departure is a collectivist notion: the *subordination* of the individual to the interests of a specific community, be that a nation, a race or a class, or possibly to the tenets of a religion. The welfare reform advanced in this study differs in essential ways from the changes any collectivist notion would suggest.

A public opinion poll conducted by Professor Richard Rose under the 'New Democracies' project in 1992 had findings that are instructive in light of what has been said so far. The researchers, analysing replies to four questions, had to decide whether the respondents' ideas were closer to an individualist view of the world or to a collectivist one. The results are shown in Figure 1. In every country, with the exception of Bulgaria and Poland, more people were inclined to take an individualist rather than a collectivist approach; in three countries two thirds of the population favoured the idea of individualism. The proportion of ambivalent positions is also significant. It cannot be said of the public opinion polls' preferences that they coincide exactly with those of this study. Nonetheless, it is remarkable that the idea of individual sovereignty and responsibility plays an important part in the value system of a considerable segment of the population in the post-socialist region.

Figure 1 **Value choices**

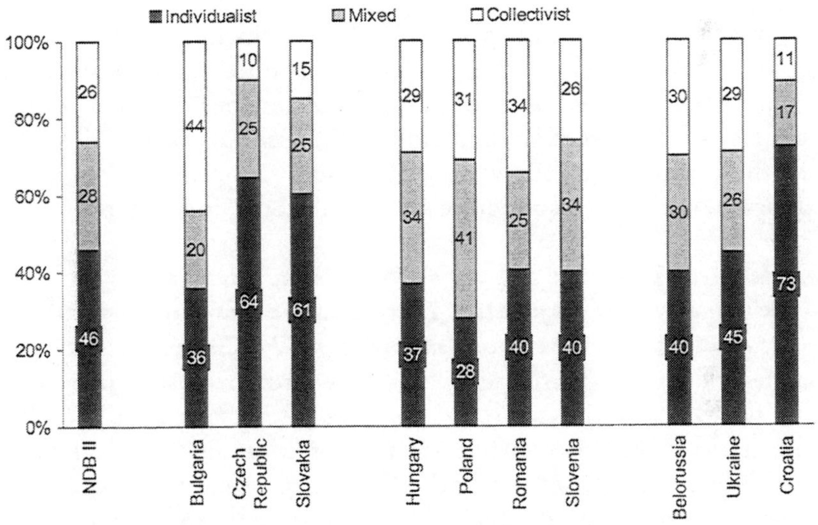

Source: Rose and Haerpfer (1993), p. 71.

Note: Those in the experiment were asked to chose from among an individualist and a collectivist alternative concerning four issues. The responses were coded as follows: Individualists: Three or four individualist preferences. Mixed: two individualist and two collectivist preferences. Collectivists: three or four collectivist preferences.

4. The Desired Features of Reformed Institutions

Let us now turn to the next plane of reform principles. The process of reform eliminates or alters old institutions, coordination mechanisms and rules of the game, and establishes new ones. Principles 3 to 7 concern what attributes these should have. To some extent these principles follow directly from Principles 1 and 2, but the desirable attributes also require some additional components.

Principle 3 (competition): The almost total monopoly of state ownership and control must cease. There must be competition among different ownership forms and co-ordination mechanisms.

Principle 3 does not prescribe quantitative proportions. It does not dictate what shares the state and non-state segments should hold. Whatever the case, the non-state sector has to attain a critical mass that can terminate the state sector's enervating position of holding a monopoly, allowing the producer (the welfare state) to dictate to the consumer. Although there are considerations of efficiency that argue in favour of competition (see Principle 4), the main source from which Principle 3 will be derived here is Principle 1. There must be competition so that citizens can choose. If they do not like what they receive from the state's institutions, they can avail themselves of non-state services as well.

The survival of the socialist system in the welfare sector has the serious consequence of leaving citizens defenceless in a number of important fields, although the decisions now come from a more diffuse 'state authority' instead of the Politburo. It depends on squabbling parties, subordinating their policy positions to their rivalry for popularity, and on the relative strength of lobbies and groups of bureaucrats reaching compromises behind the scenes, on what resources go to medical care and how much income elderly people receive. Principle 3 seeks to place a much larger fraction of decisions on these matters in the hands of the persons concerned. At least for a sizeable part of these expenditures, let them decide individually what they want to spend on their health and that of their families, how they want to prepare for their old age, and so on. This can happen if some welfare resources cease to go through the bureaucratic mechanism, funded by state tax and allocated by the state, and the households and individuals can decide about them instead through the market mechanism.

Principle 3 seeks to open up every sub-sector of the welfare sector to private, profit-seeking enterprise. It would be useful for private hospitals, clinics, health-test laboratories, kindergartens, old people's homes, and the like to emerge on a wide scale, either by founding new organisations or by privatising ones belonging to the state. The commercial insurance companies should be encouraged to expand into pension plans and medical insurance as well.

Alongside the purely state and purely for-profit private providers, there is ample scope in this sphere for founding non-state, non-profit organisations, whose owners or controllers could be societies, foundations, churches, professional associations, large employers, partnerships of smaller employers, and similar groups.

The function of applying Principle 2 (solidarity) could be shared among the state, the non-profit segment of the welfare sector, and private charitable activities.

What the public wants is security, and this the state has to provide, argue those who believe in fully nationalising the welfare sector. In my view this is a flawed argument. Sophisticated writings on uncertainty and common sense alike suggest the simple rule: do not put all your eggs in one basket. To put it in investment-portfolio terms, we should diversify. It would be a mistake, for instance, to entrust all of one's retirement savings to just one private pension fund, for if it managed the money dishonestly or unwisely, the insured would be in deep trouble. Similar problems may occur if total reliance is placed on the state. By the time a person retires, the political authorities of the day may decide to ignore the question of how much pension contribution he has paid over the years.[16] Alternatively, the pension may be eroded by surges of policy-induced inflation, and by indexation rules that whittle away at its real value (see Table 1). So the most expedient proposals for pension reform are those that rest on several pillars, allowing different pension schemes to be used concurrently.[17] Similar 'multi-pillar' solutions will be needed to fund the health service and other sub-sectors of the welfare sector.

Table 1 **The real value of pensions in the Czech Republic and Hungary**

			1990=100		
Country	1991	1992	1993	1994	1995
Czech Republic	82.9	81.2	76.9	77.5	82.2
Hungary	92.4	87.8	84.6	86.5	77.4

Sources: Czech Republic: Klimentová (1996), Chart 3; Hungary: *Figyel•*, July 11, 1996.

Public opinion is widely dispersed as to which pillars, or which combination of pillars, they prefer. The findings of the Hungarian public opinion poll mentioned earlier, presented in Table 2, show the spread of opinion well. There is a danger that parliamentary procedures, based on the majority principle, will introduce reforms that may cause one form of ownership and/or one form of control to predominate. (For instance, the *status quo*, the domination of state forms, may remain or on the contrary, a rapid and radical, total privatisation may be forced through.) In my view, Principle 1 suggests that citizens should not be forced into any particular scheme.

Table 2 **Institutional choices: support for 'state', 'market' and 'mixed' solutions (percentages)**

	Financing		
Alternatives	higher education	hospital care	pensions
Centralized state solutions	42.1	35.5	21.4
Mixed solutions	43.5	44.1	56.6
Market solutions	12.1	17.9	18.5
Unable to decide	2.2	2.5	3.5
Total	100.0	100.0	100.0

Source: Csontos, Kornai and Tóth (1996), Table 4.
Note: The Research Institute TÁRKI conducted a survey to find out how informed the Hungarian population is about the relationship between welfare services and taxation, and about the preferences concerning various institutional alternatives. The sample size was about 1000 individuals. The first alternatives represent the *status quo*, i.e. services financed and run by the state or by semi-governmental agencies, the third alternatives represent a decentralised and largely privatised welfare sector, the second incorporate multi-pillar institutional arrangements.

So far as possible, let individuals choose for themselves. There should emerge a 'menu' of various forms of ownership and mechanisms of control and co-ordination from which citizens can choose. They should be able to learn from their own and others' experience, to experiment, and to modify their points of view. That is one more reason why competition is needed in the welfare sector. In the presence of competition, selection can be made not only through the friction-ridden transmission of the political process, but also directly, through the market choices of households.

Principle 4 (incentives): Forms of ownership and control must emerge that encourage efficiency.

This principle is so self-evident it hardly needs arguing at all. The only reason for including it among the declared principles is that politicians and academics who defend the *status quo* in the welfare sector tend to forget it.

The incentives for efficiency (and here is a substantial difference from previous practice) must be given on the demand side as well to citizens, as *recipients* of welfare services. This means that with only the rarest possible exceptions, the services should not be free. Instead of having state subsidies to force the price down below the market level, there should be state assistance, targeted (by voucher form, for instance) to those for whom it is justified.[18] (This would normally mean those in need, in line with the principle of solidarity.) Even if the state or the insurer covers most of the cost of a welfare service, recipients should still contribute a co-payment, so that they can sense that the service is not free.

Proper incentives on the demand side include inducing efficiency in the insurers that finance the welfare services to a large extent. This is one of several arguments against the monopoly of the monstrous 'great wens' of the central state health insurance and pension authorities. Where there is no competition, there cannot be a sufficient incentive for efficiency and thrift.

The same argument applies on the supply side, to the organisations that provide the health, education and other services, and the care for children and the elderly. When commenting on Principle 3, I cited the sovereignty of the individual as an argument for competition. Let no one be left at the mercy of a single monopoly organisation. Competition is useful in other ways too, encouraging improvements in quality, the development of technology, the discovery and introduction of new scientific advances, and the reduction of costs.[19]

Another aspect of incentives and efficiency to consider is the most expedient form in which to accumulate and utilise 'welfare reserves'. Two pure cases can be distinguished. The first of them applies most consistently under the socialist system, when the pension system and every other welfare service are provided on a nationalized, 'pay-as-you-go' principle. Households are not expected to save for security purposes. Instead they are forced to pay the taxes that finance both all welfare services and all investment. Total centralisation leads to low efficiency, and not just in the sphere of welfare provisions. The same is well known to apply to the selection and execution of investment projects.

The other, quite opposite pure case would be one in which the accumulation of reserves was left entirely to households. Each household would place all these in a portfolio consisting of several components, allocating some deposits to the banks and mutual funds, and paying premiums to insurance companies and pension funds and so on. The financial sector, i.e. the credit and capital markets, would in turn use this huge stock of savings to finance investment in a decentralised fashion.

These two cases demonstrate the extremes of perfectly centralised and perfectly decentralised capital allocation mechanisms. While the decentralised mechanism has many advantages, we can reasonably suppose that there will be a need for some public investment financed out of taxation (e.g., to finance infrastructural investment projects or other public goods.)[20] One thing, however, has conclusively emerged from the great historic contest between the socialist and capitalist systems: a system in which decentralised investment based on private ownership and competition predominates is more efficient than one in which centralisation and state ownership prevail. Now the savings set aside for illness, unemployment, accident, or old age form such a vast proportion of total savings that it cannot be right simply to hand them to the bureaucracy. The bulk of this vast quantity of savings must be employed in a decentralised way. Following this line of argument to its conclusion, Principle 4 (incentives for efficiency), provides a further weighty argument in favour of Principle 3, the spread of competition and non-state institutions.

Principle 5 (a new role for the state): The main functions of the state in the welfare sector must be to supply legal frameworks, to supervise non-state institutions and to provide 'ultimate', last resort insurance and aid. The state undertakes the responsibility to ensure every citizen's access to basic education and health care.

To argue about whether the state's role should be 'large' or 'small', or whether it should remain in the welfare sector or withdraw from it, is a sterile debate. The essential requirement is a radical transformation of the state's role. Let us briefly review the functions of the state in a reformed welfare sector.

- By passing and enforcing the new legislation required, the state acts as guardian over the legality of the welfare sector's operation. It is most important that citizens can seek legal redress from the courts against the government and its apparatus, insurers, hospitals, doctors, old people's homes or other bodies, in cases when their rights are infringed.
- The state needs to establish suitable bodies to exercise state supervision over the welfare sector and its various sub-sectors (health care, health insurance, pension insurance, and the rest). This should be complemented by a watchdog role from claimants' and users' associations, the press, and 'civil society' as a whole.
- The state should guarantee the security of savings that citizens entrust to insurance institutions or pension funds, through a system of reinsurance.[21]
- As mentioned earlier, it is desirable that there be a role for non-state organisations in applying the principle of solidarity.

Nonetheless, there is no way the state can avoid making a substantial contribution as well. I do not agree with those who say this should be hidden away among other public expenditure, so that the voters do not notice.[22] It needs to be stated openly that state assistance is being paid to those in need, out of revenue from the taxpayers.

- Declaring that the state bears responsibility for basic education and health care still leaves open the question of how it is to be fulfilled and through what kind of institutions. It neither includes the requirement nor precludes the possibility that institutions owned or controlled by the state take part in providing the service, or the state budget contributes to financing it.

It emerges clearly from what has been said that this study does not put forward a *laissez faire* programme. It does not seek to relieve the state of its responsibility for the welfare sector, even if most of the tasks are to be performed by enterprises based on private ownership and non-profit institutions organized by various communities, and these are to be coordinated mainly by the market and spurred on by competition. This must take place under rules written by the state, and under the supervision of the state and 'civil society'. The state must also contribute its economic resources where there is an inescapable need for it to do so.

The various instances of 'market failure' have been sufficiently clarified by economists. There is justification for the state to intervene in cases where the market has failed, provided that there is no reason to fear that state activity will cause even greater failure.[23] However, in many cases it is difficult to gauge the relative chances of market and government failure. This is one reason why this study leaves open the question of the optimal size of the segment of the welfare sector that is either under state ownership or direct state control. If the public, through the political process, express a wish that part of the financial provision for old age should still come from the state pension system, that certain hospitals should remain in state ownership, and so on, and if they are willing to pay the tax to support these preferences, their wishes should be respected. The second proviso (willingness to pay the associated tax burden) leads on to the next principle.

The debates in the post-socialist countries about reforming the welfare sector have been mainly about Principles 3 and 5. The views have been widely dispersed, as in every weighty public debate. Mention has to be made of a characteristic line of argument that can be clearly discerned within the multiplicity of views. This differs from the position taken in this study in several essential respects. The underlying desire is to conserve the role and institutions of the state as they developed before the change of the political system in 1989-90. A centralised, state pension scheme, run on the 'pay-as-you-go' principle, would continue to dominate the pension system. State-owned health institutions would continue to enjoy a near-monopoly, provision of health care would be state-financed, and so on. Two main arguments are advanced for this position. One has an ethical-political nature. The market has failed to look after the poorer sections of society, which leaves the general state provisions as the only effective, and humane option. The other is economic in nature. It is cheaper to run social care organisations if they are large and centralised, and if society does not have to pay the costs of competition and a profit margin for non-state owners.

In line with the general approach in this study, I will refrain from taking issue here with these alternative positions. My views can be deduced from the exposition of the principles.

Principle 6 (transparency): The link between welfare services provided by the state and the tax burden that finances them must become apparent to citizens. The practical measures of reform must be preceded by an open and informed public debate. Politicians and political parties must declare what their welfare policies are, and how they will be financed.

The principle falls into three parts. The first sentence was inspired by realising a serious problem: citizens do not discern clearly that the costs of the services of the welfare state are borne by them, as taxpayers. Understanding the relationship between taxes and state spending is quite vague or distorted all over the world. Yet the fiscal illusions are nowhere so pronounced as in the post-socialist societies, where people have been indoctrinated for decades with the idea that health care or education is 'free'.[24] Resistance to the idea of a decentralising reform falls substantially once citizens recognise that it is the taxpayer who pays for every state service, and correctly assess the size of this payment. They have to learn that the political process gives them a choice for the welfare sector as a whole, and for all its sub-sectors separately (pensions, health care, child care, social benefits etc.), of paying through one of two channels: either by 'tax paid by household → state budget → state welfare service', or by 'insurance premium paid by household → insurer → welfare service covered by the insurer', for instance.

There is also considerable debate about the form in which the elected parliament and government of a country with a democratic political system should consult the opinion of the public *in advance* of introducing reforms, especially the opinion of groups directly affected by the measure. The answer depends on several factors, one being whether the situation requires very urgent government action. Reform of the welfare sector is not a single, short-term act. It is not designed to avert economic catastrophe or overcome an acute crisis. It entails changing the complexion of society and the relations between individuals and the state over the very long term. That is why the second part of Principle 6 states the necessity for debating these weighty reform proposals in public and providing the participants in the debate with the requisite information.

This leads to the third part of Principle 6 - the requirement of transparency of political choice. In fact, parties seldom put their ideas on the welfare sector clearly before the voters, either because they have not thought their proposals through sufficiently, or because they want to conceal their intentions.[25] This study does not fall within the sphere of political economy and the theory of public choice; it does not set out to address the question of why this is so or whether it can be changed at all. The study, in line with its normative character, puts forward requirements. The addressee of Principle 6 is the better side of every politician: if you wish to be honest with your voters, tell them frankly what you want to do about pensions, health care and the other welfare services. Other addressees are the academics researching into the subject, my colleagues and myself. We have no interest in gaining popularity; we are not running for any elected office. We have a duty to discover and demonstrate what are the gains and what are the social costs of the alternative ideas about the welfare sector. Finally, the principle is addressed to citizens. It advises them to try to discern, from the statements of politicians and the programmes of parties, what their real intentions are with the welfare sector, and to bear these in mind when voting.

In this respect it is very difficult not only to clarify intentions, but to reach a voting decision. In voting for a party or a politician, voters are choosing a 'package' of policies. A voter voting for A, rather than B, may have to overlook the fact that B's welfare policies are more attractive and decide in A's favour, because he or she prefers A's economic, judicial, foreign and other policies to B's.[26]

These very difficulties provide additional arguments for Principles 1, 3 and 5: there must be a reduction in the set of welfare services whose regulation takes place by way of the political process.

Principle 7 (the time requirement of the programme): Time must be allowed for the new institutions of the welfare sector to evolve and for citizens to adapt.

The reformed welfare sector will contain several institutions that were unknown under the socialist system. Some will be newly established, such as the new private clinics and hospitals, or the new non-state pension funds. Others will arise when the ownership form of formerly state-owned organisations is changed, for instance, when a team of doctors operates a surgery in a public hospital under a rental contract. The advocates of the reform cannot, in my view, leave these developments entirely to spontaneous processes, for many reasons. The creation of new institutions and the transformation of old ones require a careful design of new rules, which must be enacted by legislation or as by-laws of organisations. Some new organisations will emerge at the initiative of governmental agencies. In certain cases political pressure will be needed to set the process of change in motion. One might add that, by definition, a change in the role of the welfare *state* can only occur with the national state's involvement. In sum, while many components of the evolutionary process of institutional transformation will happen spontaneously, this study does not advocate a reform pattern based exclusively on spontaneous changes.[27]

At the same time I would oppose forcing through the fastest possible reform of the welfare state at any price. There are situations of crisis in which a government is compelled to enforce a painful and unpopular economic adjustment programme. Such a programme may have to include some items that cause a rapid fall in welfare spending by the state budget. That is one thing, and comprehensive reform of the welfare sector is another. The second is not fiscal fire-fighting, but a radical social transformation that cannot be conducted at breakneck speed. Sufficient time must be allowed for the programme to be carefully drafted and political support for it to be obtained.

The question of political support was mentioned under Principle 6. The better the public understands both the social costs and the likely benefits of the reform, the readier it will be to support it. If at all possible, time must be given for citizens to adapt to the new situation. The problem of differing *degrees of adaptability* lies at the heart of Principle 2. Reformers must display calm insight and patient understanding of the fact that people have different powers of adjustment.

To illustrate this, let us consider the case of reforming pensions. The younger generation can reasonably be addressed as follows. Their whole active life lies before them. Let them and their employers pay into individual accounts the sums needed for retirement, and entrust these to efficient pension funds which put them to good use. In due course their pensions will constitute the fruits of their own savings. In line with the initial postulate, Principle 1, there will be a close connection between earnings, propensity to save, and income in old age, spanning the whole life cycle.[28]

The same cannot be said to those already receiving a pension. In their case the state has to fulfil the obligations undertaken by previous governments.[29] The retired are no longer capable of adapting to a new pensions system. Apart from the state's legally defined obligations towards them, Principle 2, the principle of solidarity, also dictates that society continues applying the 'pay-as-you-go' system, whereby active members of the labour force pay tax to finance the state pensions of the inactive.

But it has to be faced that the old principle of the inter-generational bargain is going to come under increasing strain, as the tax level required to finance current pensions, coupled with their contributions to their own pension schemes, will place a considerable, and perhaps unacceptable burden, on the younger generation. Governments will therefore have to devise some kind of transitional relief through the fiscal system for the generation which faces this 'double whammy' while the 'pay-as-you-go' system is being phased out – otherwise the change of system will fall into increasing disrepute and fail to command public support.

As for the intermediate generations, I would propose they be given a choice. They should be allowed, if they so choose, to transfer their accrued state pension entitlement to their individual account at the non-state pension fund of their choice.

After these remarks about pension reform, let us return to the more general plane of discussion. As far as the state of the economy allows, the immediate sufferings caused by changes can be mitigated, and the process of adaptation encouraged, by assisting those who suffer severe losses by reform. Such individuals should receive a period of grace. Assistance without time limit should be given only to those who are really unable to adapt. For anyone else, the assistance should be granted only for a *temporary* period. Everyone must recognise that they will have to adapt to the new situation once the period of derogation is over.

5. The Desired Proportions of Allocation

Principle 8 (harmonious growth): Let there be harmonious proportions between the resources devoted to investments that directly promote rapid growth and those spent on operating and developing the welfare sector.

Two extreme views can be heard in welfare debates. One places a lopsided emphasis on the losses entailed in the transition, and fails to acknowledge that the best way to overcome the present problems is through lasting growth in the economy. However much of a truism this may be to an economist, it is constantly ignored by those who favour maintaining the welfare state *status quo*. Sometimes they scornfully dismiss the elementary economic argument that the living standard of the majority in the post-socialist countries can never be raised at least to the present average level in the West, until there is sufficient investment to produce lasting and sufficiently rapid growth.

At the other extreme is the view that tips the balance away from welfare spending and towards investment projects that contribute directly to fast growth. Statistical examinations covering several countries show that in the long term, the fastest growth has taken place in the South-East Asian countries that spend least on welfare provisions. The authors either leave Eastern European readers to draw their own conclusions, or state plainly: if you want to catch up with the West, follow the South-East Asian model.

To me, as a member of the older generation, this growth fetish sounds familiar. One of the watchwords of the Stalinist-Khrushchevite economic policy was, 'Let us catch up with the West as soon as possible.' The growth fetish led to employment of the strategy of forced growth, and to consequent distortion of the economic structure, one result of which was that people's immediate welfare needs were ignored.[30] This kind of bias led to grave problems

Table 3 **Public pension spending**

Country	Pension spending as percentage of GDP	Pension spending as percentage of government expenditure
Other than post-socialist countries (national averages by income group)		
Low	0.7 (32)	3.9 (18)
Lower-middle	2.9 (29)	10.1 (16)
Upper-middle	6.7 (20)	23.8 (13)
High	8.2 (23)	23.1 (20)
Post-socialist countries		
Albania	6.3	14.4
Bulgaria	10.2	21.5
Czech Republic	8.3	–
Hungary	11.6	18.3
Poland	14.7	29.2
Romania	6.4	14.9
Russia	6.0	–
Slovakia	9.3	18.0
Ukraine	7.1	14.8

Sources: For other than post-socialist countries: The World Bank (1994), p. 103. For post-socialist countries: UNICEF (1994), pp. 96–97.
Note: In the first part of the table the data refer to the period 1985–92 and those in parentheses indicate the number of countries for which data are available. The data for post-socialist countries refer to 1992. The figure for Russia is an estimate.

within the socialist system, whose consequences have not been overcome to this day. It would be a shame to start this all over again.

A different conclusion is reached if the international comparison is based not on the relationship between welfare spending and *rate* of growth, but rather between welfare spending and *level* of economic development. As a country progresses in economic development, so state spending on health, education, culture, and care of children and the aged increases. The connection is not deterministic, because it is affected by several other factors as well: the political complexions of governments, the country's cultural traditions, and so on. Still, there is a close relationship between overall economic development and governmental spending on human welfare. This linkage is demonstrated in Table 3.

Departure from the desirable proportion between government welfare expenditure and the level of development might occur in both directions: too much or too little spending. As an 'overcompensation' for the industrial and military excesses of the Stalinist period, some socialist countries, at a later stage in their economic development, let welfare spending run away. Prompted by the paternalist ideology and a desire to calm the population, the state undertook greater obligations than its resources warranted at that economic level. Some East European countries overreached themselves not only in the obligations undertaken by the state, but also in their fulfilment. That is why I called them 'premature welfare states' in an earlier study of mine.[31] Hungary went the furthest in this respect (see Table 4).

There is a vital need to restore the proper balance, by approaching the problem from two directions. State commitments, and entitlements from the state, must be reduced, while economic growth is promoted.

For my part, I would not venture to put forward a quantitative golden rule that would ensure harmonious proportions. It would be an exciting research task to reconsider this field in the context of the post-socialist transformation. However, although Principle 8 may not supply a method of quantification, it certainly contains a warning against allowing blatant distortions and heeding false political slogans.

Table 4 **Composition of public social expenditures in Hungary and in selected OECD countries (as percentage of GDP)**

Spending on:	Hungary 1992	Germany 1990	Spain 1989	Sweden 1991
Pensions	10.4	9.6	7.9	13.2
Health[a]	5.3	9.1	6.5	8.8
Family	3.9	1.3	0.1	1.4
Housing	2.8	0.2	0.1	0.9
Unemployment	2.3	2.1	3.1	4.1
Total	24.7	22.3	16.3	26.4

Source: OECD (1995), p. 49.
Note: Pensions include old age, disability and survivors. Unemployment includes all active programmes and unemployment compensation.
[a] Refers to 1991 and only to public sector expenditures on health.

Here I must refer back to Principle 1. One reason why more of the economic choice has to be entrusted to individuals is the doubt about whether central planners are capable of reaching an appropriate decision about these fundamental proportions. Must the state intervene in the main allocation proportions to 'defend' health care and education from the decisions of households, lest they spend too much on building factories, for instance? I hardly think there is a danger of that. On the contrary, one could expect it to emerge from the individual decisions, when aggregated on a national level, that society's voluntary, decentralised decision-making was causing it to spend *more* on health, education, and other activities in the welfare sector, than central planners would devote to them.[32] One sound argument for intervention is the fear that without a certain measure of state redistribution, guided by the solidarity criterion of Principle 2, an extremely decentralised decision-making process might fail to provide the lowest, most disadvantaged strata of society with basic welfare provisions.

Principle 9 (sustainable financing): The state budget must be continuously capable of financing the fulfilment of the state's obligations.

While Principle 8 concerns the desirable allocation of real resources, this principle draws attention to the financial aspects. However self-evident this requirement may seem, it was its infringement that ended the treatment of the welfare state as sacred in many countries.

Several economies show a substantial budget deficit, including the post-socialist countries, almost without exception. Where the budgetary system clearly earmarks revenues designed to cover specific welfare expenditures, the financial deficit of some sub-sectors of the welfare sector can be discerned, at least in part.[33] The deficit has already appeared, or the projections suggest it is likely to appear as an explosion sooner or later. In some other sub-sectors of such countries, and in the overall state welfare sector of some other countries, the funds required to defray welfare services are not separated from those covering other expenditures. State welfare expenditures are paid out of general tax revenues. Therefore it is difficult to determine the relative role of welfare spending in generating overall fiscal deficit.

This study is not intended to analyse specifically the various causes of fiscal deficit at different times and in different countries. Nonetheless, it is certainly worth drawing emphatic attention to the calculations that show how the welfare commitments legally enshrined in a certain country will become unsustainable sooner or later, other circumstances being equal, and taking into account the likely economic growth rate and demographic trends. State pension systems in particular are threatened everywhere by fiscal crisis. State health services too, with the great pressure upon them from the demand side, look as if they will eventually become impossible to finance. It varies from country to country when exactly the experts predict that the system will reach its financing limits, and whether the gap can be bridged by raising taxes. The latter is partly an economic question — higher taxes will dampen incentives and impede investment — and partly a political one — the unpopularity of tax rises must be weighed against the unfavourable effects on opinion of reducing welfare spending. Ultimately it would seem that in most post-socialist countries, the need to improve the fiscal balance will eventually force reductions in state welfare spending.

Although I have left Principles 8 and 9 to the end of the discussion, they are no less cogent than the other principles. I think the established parameters for the debates on reforming the welfare sector have become untenable. Here I refer only to the discussion in academic circles. Defenders of the welfare state rightly describe in dramatic terms the sufferings of the destitute and disadvantaged, but superciliously dismiss any mention of the requirement of harmonious economic proportions. That is no concern of theirs. Those are just narrow-minded 'fiscal' arguments that no compassionate person would consider. Alternatively, one can read economic arguments, in which a paragraph is devoted to the need for a 'social safety net', but the authors fail to think through all the social consequences of the rules they propose. Both sides usually refrain from supporting their positions with ethical considerations. I think it is high time to insist on a synthesis of outlook in ourselves and others. Neither side has a right to espouse social criteria or economic arguments alone.

6. Conclusion

The ensemble of the nine principles does not constitute a rigorous theoretical edifice, built in an axiomatic fashion. Further analysis is required to decide to what extent the various pairs and sub-sets of principles are reconcilable and to what extent they are conflicting, i.e. they have trade-off relations. For instance, Principle 1 (individual freedom and responsibility) and Principle 5 (the responsibility of the state) are not irreconcilable, although clearly the further one takes one, the less scope remains for the other.

Given such trade-offs, no prior theoretical consideration can preclude the need to make a specific, responsible choice in each case. I would like to believe it was worthwhile to have made a systematic review of principles. The system in which the principles appear and the way they are summed up, as I mentioned in the introduction, have to serve as a *memento*, a checklist, designed to prevent any principle being forgotten, when actual programmes, legislation and regulations are drafted, evaluated and enacted. Even where decision-makers are obliged to make a concession on some principle, let them do so consciously, wrestling with their conscience and common sense before reaching a compromise. Those who truly espouse the principles proposed in the study will refrain from an extreme interpretation of any of them, if it conflicts with another.[34]

The choice of subject for the study may elicit the following counter-argument. The scope for reform is given in all post-socialist countries, but it is constrained by the economic and political conditions. The latter ultimately determine what kind of reform can be implemented. If reformers really want to fight for their ideas, they will have to make concessions. They may even have to manipulate public opinion. It is not always in their interests to declare clearly and unambiguously what principles they follow, what they intend and what consequences it will have.

The fate of reforms is generally known to be decided in the political arena. Among the tasks of the academic research, I consider it important to examine the chances of welfare reform from the angle of political economy.[35] I have tried to do this in other works of mine, taking a positive political economy approach to the problem. However, I hope it will prove useful, as a complement to such positive research, to approach the issue from the opposite end as well.

The question most worth asking is not just how we can and must take the next steps, starting from where we now stand. It is also vitally important to ask where we really want to go. Particularly in the case of the welfare sector, it is worth considering the *desired terminal state*, because the answer is highly debatable and indeterminate in historical terms, and because, as I have said already, there is no country to serve as a real model, a pattern that we might wish to follow.

The nine principles expounded in the study are not tied to any particular party, in Hungary or elsewhere in the post-socialist region. They cannot be pigeon-holed in the usual way. They are neither 'left-wing' nor 'right-wing', or to use American terminology, they do not correspond with what the traditional 'liberal' or 'conservative' ideas would suggest. They are dissociated from the earlier strand of social democracy, which saw as its main task the fullest possible construction of a welfare *state*, and which bears the historical blame for the exorbitant lengths to which this was taken. The study also dissociates itself both from the cold-hearted radicalism that would dismantle all the achievements of the welfare state, and from the ideologues who are uncritically biased against the state and in favour of the market. The set of nine principles represents a specific 'centrist' position, and though dissociated from the traditional left and right wings, draws noteworthy ideas and proposals from both. My motive in doing so is not to make both sides like what I say. That might well rebound, so that neither side liked the proposal. I have drawn up these nine principles in the belief that this particular set form an integral whole.

The approach underlying this paper is akin to that of many other authors in political and academic life alike. Perhaps it is not too soon to claim that this constitutes an international trend – though one which has not yet found an apposite name for its view of the world. It has both feet planted in capitalism. It does not seek a 'third way'. It does, however, seek – not just with empty wishes, but by building up appropriate institutions – to ensure that capitalism has something more than a human face: a human heart and mind as well. It seeks to build much more firmly on individual responsibility, the market, competition, private ownership, and the profit motive. On the other hand, it does not accept any of the East European variants of ultra-conservatism. It seeks to apply the principle of solidarity not simply through individual charitable action. Within certain bounds it is prepared to countenance state redistribution for this purpose. It has no illusions about the market, and it does not reject all state intervention out of hand. But it does reject the proliferation of bureaucracy and centralisation to which old style social democracy was so addicted.

The historical experiences of the future will decide what effect this emerging intellectual and political trend will have on the transformation of the welfare sector.

Finally, it is worth stressing that the purpose of this study is not to narrow down the scope of the welfare sector, nor to promote a cut in the resources available for health care, education, care for children and the elderly and other welfare tasks. The approach here differs from the line taken in the welfare state of the socialist period in advocating that only part of the expenditure on welfare be covered by taxation. Furthermore, the decisions about this part are to be taken by a democratic political process, not by the whim of the planners. The rest of the expenditure, a much higher proportion than hitherto, will be determined directly, by the voluntary decisions of households. Ultimately, this will result in welfare expenditure that is greater in volume and more accurately targeted than before.

References

Andorka, Rudolf, Anna Kondratas and István György Tóth (1994) *Hungary's Welfare State in Transition: Structure, Initial Reforms and Recommendations*, Policy Study No. 3 of The Joint Hungarian-International Blue Ribbon Commission, Indianapolis, Indiana: The Hudson Institute and Budapest: Institute of Economics.

Atkinson, Anthony B., and John Micklewright (1992) *Economic Transformation in Eastern Europe and the Distribution of Income*, Cambridge University Press.

Beattie, Roger, and Warren McGillivray (1995) 'A Risky Strategy: Reflections on the World Bank Report "Averting the old age crisis"' *ISSA Review*, 48 (3-4).

Berlin, Isaiah (1969) *Four Essays on Liberty*, London: Oxford University Press.

Buchanan, James M. (1986) *Liberty, Market and the State: Political Economy in the 1980s*, Brighton: Wheatsheaf Books.

Buchanan, James M., and Tullock, Gordon (1962) *The Calculus of Consent: Logical Foundations of Constitutional Democracy*, Ann Arbor: University of Michigan Press.

Csontos, László, János Kornai, and István György Tóth (1996) 'What Citizens Think About Taxes and Reform of the Welfare System. The Lessons of a Questionnaire-Based Survey Taken in Hungary', Mimeo. Budapest: CEU, Collegium Budapest and TÁRKI.

Culpitt, Ian, (1992) *Welfare and Citizenship: Beyond the Crisis of the Welfare State*, London and Newbury Park, CA: Sage.

Davis, Lance E., and Douglas C. North (1971) *Institutional Change and American Economic Growth*, Cambridge University Press.

Diamond, Peter (1996) 'Government provision and regulation of economic support in old age', in *Annual World Bank Conference on Development Economics 1995*, Washington, D.C.: The World Bank, pp. 83-103.

Goldstein, Ellen, Alexander S. Preker, Olusoji Adeyi, and Gnanaraj Chellaraj (1996) *Trends in Health Status, Services and Finance: The Transition in Central and Eastern Europe. Volume I*, World Bank Technical Paper No. 341. Washington, D.C.: The World Bank.

James, Estelle (1996) *Protecting the Old and Promoting Growth. A Defence of 'Averting the Old Age Crisis'*, Policy Research Working Paper, No. 1570. Washington, D.C.: The World Bank, January.

Klimentová, Jana (1996) 'Possibilities of the Transformation of the Financing of Pension Insurance in the Czech Republic', Mimeo. Prague: Ministry of Labour and Social Affairs.

Kornai, János (1972) *Rush versus Harmonic Growth*, Amsterdam: North-Holland.

Kornai, János (1992) 'The postsocialist transition and the state: Reflections in the light of Hungarian fiscal problems', *American Economic Review*, Papers and Proceedings, 82 (2): 1-21.

Kornai, János (1997) 'Reform of the Welfare Sector in the Post-Communist Countries: A Normative Approach', in *Transforming Post-Communist Political Economies*, Joan M. Nelson, Charles Tilly and Lee Walker (eds.), Washington D.C., National Academy Press, pp. 272-298.

Lindbeck, Assar (1996) 'Incentives in the Welfare-State, Lessons for Would-Be Welfare States', Seminar Paper, No. 604, Stockholm: Institute for International Economic Studies, Stockholm University, January.

Lindbeck, Assar, and Jörgen W. Weibull (1987) 'Strategic Interaction with Altruism: The Economics of Fait Accompli', Seminar Paper, No. 376, Stockholm: Institute for International Economic Studies, University of Stockholm.

Lindbeck, Assar, Per Molander, Torsten Persson, Olof Petersson, Agnar Sandmo, Birgitta Swedenborg, and Niels Thygesen (1994) *Turning Sweden Around*, Cambridge, MA and London: The MIT Press.

Milanovic, Branko (1996) 'Income, Inequality, and Poverty During the Transition', Mimeo. Washington, D.C.: The World Bank, August.

Nelson, Joan M. (1992) 'Poverty, equity, and the politics of adjustment', in *The Politics of Economic Adjustment*, Stephan Haggard, and Robert R. Kaufman, eds. Princeton: Princeton University Press, pp. 221-269.

Niskanen, William A. (1971) *Bureaucracy and Representative Government*, Chicago: Aldine-Atherton.

North, Douglas C. (1990) *Institutions, Institutional Change and Economic Performance*, Cambridge: Cambridge University Press.

Nozick, Robert (1974) *Anarchy, State and Utopia*, New York: Basic Books.

OECD (1995) *Hungary*, OECD Economic Surveys. September, Paris: OECD.

Rawls, John (1971) *A Theory of Justice*, Cambridge, MA: Harvard University Press.

Rose, Richard, and Christian Haerpfer (1993) *Adapting to Transformation in Eastern Europe: New Democracies Barometer—II*, Studies in Public Policy, No. 212, Centre for the Study of Public Policy, University of Strathclyde, Glasgow.

Sen, Amartya (1973) *On Economic Inequality*, Oxford: Clarendon Press and New York: Norton.

Sen, Amartya (1990) 'Individual freedom as a social commitment', Acceptance speech at the award ceremony for the second Senator Giovanni Agnelli International Prize in 1990, published by the Agnelli Foundation and also in *The New York Review of Books*, June 14, 1990, pp. 49-54.

Sen, Amartya (1992) *Inequality Reexamined*, New York: Russell Sage Foundation and Cambridge, MA: Harvard University Press.

Sen, Amartya (1996) 'Social commitment and democracy: The demands of equity and financial conservatism', in *Living as Equals*, Paul Barker (ed.) Oxford: Oxford University Press, pp. 9-38

Sipos, Sándor (1994) 'Income transfers: Family support and poverty relief', in *Labour Markets and Social Policy in Central and Eastern Europe. The Transition and Beyond*, Nicholas Barr, ed. Published for the World Bank. Oxford: Oxford University Press, pp. 226-259.

Tullock, Gordon (1965) *The Politics of Bureaucracy*, Washington, D.C.: Public Affairs Press.

UNICEF (1994) *Crisis in Mortality, Health and Nutrition. Central and Eastern Europe in Transition, Public Policy and Social Conditions*, Economies in Transition

Studies, Regional Monitoring Report, Florence, Italy: UNICEF, International Child Development Centre (ICDC).

The World Bank (1994) *Averting the Old Age Crisis*, The World Bank Policy Research Report, Oxford: Oxford University Press, published for the World Bank.

The World Bank (1995a) *Hungary: Structural Reforms for Sustainable Growth*, First draft. Document of the World Bank, Country Operations Division, Central Europe Department, Report No. 3577-HU, February 10, Washington, D.C.

The World Bank (1995b) *Hungary: Structural Reforms for Sustainable Growth*, Document of the World Bank, Country Operations Division, Central Europe Department, Report No. 13577-HU, June 12, Washington, D.C.

Notes

[1] Many authors take the welfare functions linked with unemployment (unemployment insurance and benefits, retraining, and so on) to be part of the welfare sector. Others prefer to discuss this subject in the context of the economic, social and political problems of the labour market. This depends on whether the definition of the welfare sector's tasks is intended to cover the rights and duties of *citizens* in general, or extend specially to the problems of the *workers* as well. Any thorough study of the relationship between the welfare services, the role of the state and the problem of unemployment would require a careful analysis of macro-economic issues, e.g. investment and growth. That would go certainly beyond the space constraint of the paper.

[2] The welfare system in socialist countries outside Europe, notably China, differed greatly from the type found in the countries mentioned. This study deals solely with the post-socialist transition in the former Soviet Union and Eastern Europe.

[3] Why nine? I do not claim that this set of principles embodies some kind of whole. Perhaps some principle or other could be omitted, or others added to the set. The text could be expressed otherwise, even if the discussion were confined to those who more or less endorse the position taken in the study, at least in their overall view of the world. The author is certainly relieved to have stopped at nine, avoiding any hint of 'ten commandments'.

[4] The study is a product of a comprehensive research project, directed by the author, in which several participants reviewed the state of the Hungarian welfare sector, international experience, and debated on the reform in Hungary and abroad. They also made practical proposals for reform. The groundwork of principle was followed by practical proposals on the specific sub-sectors (pensions, health, allowances, and so on).

[5] I have tried to produce a 'minimalist' solution, in other words, I want to present the least requirement, only as much as seems necessary and sufficient as an ethical starting point for welfare reform.

[6] Numerous authors have dealt with the interpretation of individual freedom. The study by Isaiah Berlin (1969) is especially important for applying the distinction between positive and negative liberty. The negative freedom of the individual is threatened by a hyperactive, disproportionate, paternalist welfare state. It would be desirable for society to develop in a direction that protects and reinforces individuals' negative freedom while concurrently enhancing their positive freedom. In this sense Amartya Sen (1990)

considers the assertion of individual freedom to be an obligation upon society. See also Sen (1996).

[7] A representative survey in Hungary, taken at the author's initiative, sought to gauge the public's attitude towards reforming the welfare sector (see Csontos, Kornai and Tóth, 1996). One question was, 'How are you preparing for your old age?' The answer from 51% of respondents was that they had not thought about it yet. It seems desirable to establish institutions that induce everyone, in line with Principle 1, to be mainly responsible themselves for what happens to them in the future.

[8] On the issue of social assistance and other redistributive measures see Andorka, Kondratas and Tóth (1994), Atkinson and Micklewright (1992), Milanovic (1996) and Sipos (1994).

[9] Warnings sound during the debates in Eastern Europe that the financial situation of the earlier middle class, especially some of those in intellectual occupations, has deteriorated fast. Action to prevent this deterioration can be justified by the principle of solidarity. This should take the form not of benefits, but of support for adaptation: occupational retraining, and changing jobs and homes, according to the requirements of the new employment structure.

[10] Let us leave open here the question of how specifically to define 'basic needs', what foodstuffs it should include, what kind of housing, and what health care. This can obviously not be decided without reference to the level of economic development in the country concerned.

[11] Much perplexity has been caused by confounding risk-sharing insurance, which can be placed on a commercial basis, with assistance based on altruistic solidarity. It is particularly confusing when the two become mingled in the definition of so-called 'social insurance'.

[12] An example is the pension debt in many countries, which is likely to reach an unsustainable scale in the future. Hungary's pension debt in 1994, for instance, were equivalent to 263% of GDP (see World Bank, 1995a, p. 36 and 1995b, p. 127).

[13] Another weighty argument is that public education has a substantial external utility, apart from its use to the individual.

[14] See Lindbeck and Weibull (1987).

[15] To single out a few, especially influential works from the vast literature on the subject: Berlin (1969), Buchanan (1986), Nozick (1974), Rawls (1971), and Sen (1973), (1992). For a broad survey on the debate about the philosophical ramifications of the modern welfare state see Culpitt (1992). Although Culpitt favours the preservation of the status quo, the survey presents a balanced exposition of the main pro and con arguments.

[16] This applies in most post-socialist countries today. The 'pay-as-you-go' system and the repeated changes in pension rules, coupled with the tendencies to level out pensions, have left a very loose correlation between the actual pension and the pension premium contributed during the active phase of the pensioner's lifetime.

[17] The new Hungarian Pension Reform Act of 1997, and also the recent proposals elaborated by the Czech and Polish Government and by the Hungarian Ministry of Finance are based also on 'multi-pillar' considerations. For an excellent survey and

careful proposals see the World Bank's report *Averting the Old Age Crisis* (1994). For a critical assessment of the World Bank report see Beattie and McGillivray (1995), and the rejoinder by the principal author, James (1996). The World Bank proposals are analyzed and criticized also in Diamond (1996).

[18] A debate is going on the advantages and disadvantages of vouchers in welfare provisions. For a survey see Culpitt (1992).

[19] I realise that both for-profit and non-state, non-profit insurers and providers may try to cut costs at the expense of recipients (the sick, or the child or old person requiring the provision). However, the same may occur with state ownership and control as well, unless money is super-abundant in the state sector. Unlimited expansion of costs versus savings at the expense of those receiving the services are the horns of one of the welfare sector's gravest dilemmas. I do not feel competent to respond reassuringly to the questions this raises, and even an attempt would require a separate study.

[20] There has been detailed discussion in economic writings about the cases in which state selection, financing and/or implementation of investment is justified.

[21] Presumably some kind of non-state or quasi-state reinsurance institutions can be established to give adequate protection to the insurance investments of citizens against a failure of a particular insurer. It will suffice if the state provides a guarantee of last resort, should the reinsurer be unable to cover the loss. The function of an 'ultimate insurer' is still a fiscal burden, but a much smaller one than financing the entire provisions.

[22] Most people have a sense of solidarity with the community. The Hungarian poll mentioned several times (Csontos, Kornai and Tóth, 1996) showed many childless respondents still willing to pay the tax to support higher education.

[23] Public choice theory and research on bureaucracies (see Buchanan and Tullock, 1962, Niskanen, 1971, and Tullock, 1965) explain the conditions and consequences of various forms of government failure.

[24] The survey taken in Hungary, referred to earlier several times (Csontos, Kornai and Tóth, 1996), revealed, for instance, that only a fifth of the respondents could estimate within a ±25% margin of error what tax burden was imposed by ostensibly free state health care. The rest of the sample either gave guesses even further from the truth, or could not answer the question at all.

[25] Complete disregard for Principle 6 belonged to the essence of the socialist system. By comparison, the democratic system of state has made great progress in applying the principle. There can be few illusions, however, about how consistently the principle applies in the actual practice of parliamentary democracy.

[26] It would exceed the scope of this study to discuss how far this problem might be resolved by a system of referenda on most important legislation. Except in a few countries, democratic constitutions only allow political decisions to be put to a referendum in exceptional cases.

[27] These remarks are compatible with the theory of institutional innovation and the evolutionary perception of the history of changing economic institutions (see Davis and North, 1971 and North, 1990).

[28] As I explained when discussing Principles 3 and 5, I think it would be wrong to refuse from the outset, even for young people, to have a state pension 'pillar' as well, applying to all, alongside the other 'pillars' of pension insurance. This must be kept if the majority of the population feel it enhances their sense of security, and declare their willingness to fund it through taxation. Sooner or later, however, it will be expedient to reach a situation where state pensions cover only the smaller part of retirement incomes.
[29] The Hungarian parliament enacted the new, reformed pension system in 1997. This act is more or less akin in its spirit with the normative principles espoused in this study and the remark presented in note 28.
[30] Twenty-five years ago, I published my study *Rush versus Harmonic Growth* (Kornai, 1972), which argued against this growth fetish.
[31] Kornai (1992).
[32] This seems to be confirmed by experience under the socialist system. The iron hand of Stalinist economic policy ensured that the state did not 'overspend' on hospitals, housing etc., concentrating resources on developing heavy industry and increasing military might instead.
[33] In Hungary, for instance, the state pension system and medical care has to be financed from two kinds of social-security contribution.
[34] According to press reports (for instance in *The New York Times*, October 15, 1996), the homeless are to be deported from Moscow, and some of them forced into accommodation reminiscent of internment camps, outside the capital. If the report is true, this will put a roof over the heads of the homeless and ease the lives of others in an overcrowded city. On the other hand, this paternalist measure, applied in an especially brutal form, is a grave breach of Principle 1: the sovereignty of the individual and his or her fundamental human rights.
[35] On the political economy of reforming the welfare state, and/or cutting governmental social transfers see Lindbeck et al. (1994), and Lindbeck (1996) discussing the Swedish experience and Nelson (1992) analyzing the problems of some countries in Latin-America, Asia and Africa.

SMF Papers

1. *The Social Market Economy*
   Robert Skidelsky
   £3.50
   1989

2. *Responses to Robert Skidelsky on the Social Market Economy*
   Sarah Benton, Kurt Biedenkopf, Frank Field, Danny Finkelstein, Francis Hawkings, Graham Mather
   £3.50
   1989

3. *Europe Without Currency Barriers*
   Samuel Brittan, Michael Artis
   £5.00
   1989

4. *Greening the White Paper*
   Gwyn Bevan, Marshall Marinker
   £2.00
   1989

5. *Education and the Labour Market*
   Adrian Wooldridge
   £5.00
   1990

6. *Crisis in Eastern Europe: Roots and Prospects*
   Robin Okey
   £4.00
   1990

7. *Fighting Fiscal Privilege: Towards a Fiscal Constitution*
   Deepak Lal
   £4.00
   1990

8. *Eastern Europe in Transition*
   Clive Crook, Daniel Franklin
   £5.00
   1990

9. *The Open Network and its Enemies: Towards a Contestable Telecommunications Market*
   Daniel Finkelstein, Craig Arnall
   £2.00
   1990

10. *A Restatement of Economic Liberalism*
Samuel Brittan
£5.00
1990

11. *Standards in Schools: Assessment, Accountability, and the Purposes of Education*
John Marks
£6.00
1991

12. *Deeper Share Ownership*
Matthew Gaved, Anthony Goodman
£3.00
1992

13. *Fighting Leviathan*
Howard Davies
£6.00
1992

14. *The Age of Entitlement*
David Willetts
£6.00
1993

15. *Schools and the State*
Evan Davis
£6.00
1993

16. *Public Sector Pay: In Search of Sanity*
Ron Beadle
£4.00
1993

17. *Beyond Next Steps: a civil service for the 1990s*
Sir Peter Kemp
£4.00
1993

18. *Post Communist Societies in Transition: A Social Market Perspective*
John Gray
£4.00
1994

19. *Two Cheers for the Institutions*
Stanley Wright
£5.00
1994

20. *Civic Conservatism*
David Willetts
£5.00
1994

21. *The Undoing of Conservatism*
John Gray
£5.00
1994

22. *Meritocracy and the 'Classless Society'*
Adrian Wooldridge
£8.00
1995

23. *Public Spending into the Millenium*
Nick Bosanquet
£5.00
1995

24. *Communities in the Countryside*
Damian Green
£10.00
1996

25. *The Ties that Bind Us*
Matthew d'Ancona
£10.00
1996

26. *The Prospects for Public Spending*
Andrew Tyrie
£7.50
1996

27. *Taxing and Spending Dilemmas*
Norman Gemmell
£10.00
1997

28. *Making Shoplifters Pay*
Joshua Bamfield
£12.00
1997

29. *Britain's Relative Economic Decline 1870-1995*
Nicholas Crafts
£6.00
1997

30. *Beyond the Welfare State*
Robert Skidelsky
£8.00
1997

31. *Lessons from the Republicans*
Tim Hames, Alan Grant
£12.00
1997

32. *Reforming Welfare*
Frank Field
£5.00
1997

33. *Dilemmas in Modern Healthcare*
John Spiers (ed.)
£10.00
1997

34. *Ready for Treatment*
Nick Bosanquet, Stephen Pollard
£5.00
1997

35. *The Future of Welfare*
Roderick Nye (ed.)
£10.00
1998

36. *Welfare to Work*
David Willetts
£10.00
1998

37. *Back on Target*
Nick Bosanquet, Tony Hockley
£10.00
1998

38. *The State of the Future*
Robert Skidelsky (ed.)
£10.00
1998

39. *Reflections on Welfare Reform*
Frank Field
£10.00
1998

40. *The Purpose of Politics*
Oliver Letwin
£8.00
1999

41. *A Cue for Change*
Oliver Morgan
£12.00
1999

42. *The Social Market and the State*
Ed. Alastair Kilmarnock
£12.99
1999

43. *A Question of Choice*
Stephen Pollard & Katharine Raymond
£10.00
1999

44. *The Sex-Change Society*
Melanie Phillips
£12.99
1999

Reports

1. *Environment, Economics and Development after the 'Earth Summit'*
Andrew Cooper
£3.00
1992

2. *Another Great Depression? Historical lessons for the 1990s*
Robert Skidelsky, Liam Halligan
£5.00
1993

3. *Exiting the Underclass: Policy towards America's urban poor*
Andrew Cooper, Catherine Moylan
£5.00
1993

4. *Britain's Borrowing Problem*
Bill Robinson
£5.00
1993

Occasional Papers

1. *Deregulation*
   David Willetts
   £3.00
   1993

2. *'There is no such thing as society'*
   Samuel Brittan
   £3.00
   1993

3. *The Opportunities for Private Funding in the NHS*
   David Willetts
   £3.00
   1993

4. *A Social Market for Training*
   Howard Davies
   £3.00
   1993

5. *Beyond Unemployment*
   Robert Skidelsky, Liam Halligan
   £6.00
   1993

6. *Brighter Schools*
   Michael Fallon
   £5.00
   1993

7. *Understanding 'Shock Therapy'*
   Jeffrey Sachs
   £8.00
   1994

8. *Recruiting to the Little Platoons*
   William Waldegrave
   £6.00
   1994

9. *The Culture of Anxiety: The Middle Class Crisis*
   Matthew Symonds
   £4.00
   1994

10. *What is left of Keynes?*
    Samuel Brittan, Meghnad Desai, Deepak Lal
    Robert Skidelsky, Tom Wilson
    £8.00
    1994

11. *Winning the Welfare Debate*
Peter Lilley (Introduction by Frank Field)
£8.00
1995

12. *Financing the Future of the Welfare State*
Robert Skidelsky, Will Hutton
£5.00
1995

13. *Picking Winners: The East Asian Experience*
Ian Little
£8.00
1996

14. *Over-the-Counter Medicines*
Alan Maynard, Gerald Richardson
£5.00
1996

15. *Pressure Group Politics in Modern Britain*
William Waldegrave, Charles Secrett, Peter Bazalgette
Adam Gaines, Kate Parminter (Introduction by Peter Riddell)
£10.00
1996

16. *Design Decisions: Improving the Public Effectiveness of Public Purchasing*
Various authors
£5.00
1996

17. *Stakeholding Society vs Enterprise Centre of Europe*
Robert Skidelsky, Will Hutton
£3.00
1997

18. *Setting Enterprise Free*
Ian Lang
£3.00
1997

19. *Community Values and the Market Economy*
John Kay
£10.00
1997

Other Papers

Local Government and the Social Market
George Jones
£3.00
1991

Full Employment without Inflation
James Meade
£6.00
1994

Memoranda

1. *Provider Choice: 'Opting In' through the Private Finance Initiative*
Michael Fallon
£2.00
1993

2. *The Importance of Resource Accoutning*
Evan Davis
£2.00
1993

3. *Why There is No Time to Teach: What is wrong with the National Curriculum 10 Level Scale*
John Marks
£5.00
1994

4. *All Free Health Care Must be Effective*
Brendan Devlin, Gwyn Bevan
£2.00
1994

5. *Recruting to the Little Platoons*
William Waldegrave
£2.00
1994

6. *Labour and the Public Services*
John Willman
£5.00
1994

7. *Organising Cost Effective Access to Justice*
Gwyn Bevan, Tony Holland and Michael Partington
£5.00
1994

8. *A Memo to Modernisers*
Ron Beadle, Andrew Cooper, Evan Davis, Alex de Mont
Stephen Pollard, David Sainsbury, John Willman
£3.00
1994

9. *Consevatives in Opposition: Republicans in the US*
Daniel Finkelstein
£3.00
1994

10. *Housing Benefit: Incentives for Reform*
Greg Clark
£3.00
1994

11. *The Market and Clause IV*
Stephen Pollard
£1.00
1994

12. *Yeltsin's Choice: Background to the Chechenya Crisis*
Vladimir Mau
£3.00
1994

13. *Teachers' Practices: A New Model for State Schools*
Tony Meredith
£3.00
1994

14. *The Right to Earn: Learning to Live with Top People's Pay*
Ron Beadle
£5.00
1995

15. *A Memo to Modernisers II*
John Abbott, Peter Boone, Tom Chandos, Evan Davis,
Alex de Mont, Ian Pearson MP, Stephen Pollard,
Katharine Raymond, John Spiers
£3.00
1995

16. *Schools, Selection and the Left*
Stephen Pollard
£3.00
1995

17. *The Future of Long-Term Care*
Andrew Cooper, Roderick Nye
£3.00
1995

18. *Better Job Options for Disabled People: Re-employ and Beyond*
Peter Thurnham
£3.00
1995

19. *Negative Equity and the Housing Market*
Andrew Cooper, Roderick Nye
£1.00
1995

20. *Industrial Injuries Compensation: Incentives to Change*
Greg Clark, Iain Smedley
£3.00
1995

21. *Better Government by Design: Improving the Effectiveness of Public Purchasing*
Katharine Raymond, Marc Shaw
£5.00
1996

22. *A Memo to Modernisers III*
Evan Davis, John Kay, Alex de Mont, Stephen Pollard
Brian Pomeroy, Katharine Raymond
£5.00
1996

23. *The Citizen's Charter Five Years On*
Roderick Nye
£3.00
1996

24. *Standards of English and Maths for Primary Schools in 1995*
John Marks
£10.00
1997

25. *Standards of Reading, Spelling & Maths for 7 year olds*
In Primary Schools for 1995
John Marks
£10.00
1997

26. *An Expensive Lunch: The Political Economy*
of Britain's New Monetary Framework
Robert Chote
£3.00
1997

27. *A Memo to Martin Taylor*
David Willetts
£5.00
1997

28. *Why Fundholding Must Stay*
David Colin-Thomé
£2.00
1997

29. *Lessons from Wisconsin's Welfare Reform*
J. Jean Rogers
£5.00
1997

30. *The Sex Change State*
Melanie Phillips
£4.00
1997

31. *Freedom & the Family*
William Hague
£3.00
1998

32. *Practical Road Pricing*
Stephen Glaister
£5.00
1998

33. *New Dynamics in Public Health Policy*
Nick Bosanquet & Tony Hockley
£5.00
1998

34. *Education Action Zones: The Conditions of Success*
Robert Skidelsky & Katharine Raymond
£8.00
1998

35. *An Anatomy of Failure: Standards in English Schools for 1997*
John Marks
£10.00
1998

36. *Beyond the PSBR: Auditing the New Public Finances*
Evan Davis, Brian Pomeroy
£3.00
1998

37. *Wanted: A New Consumer Affairs Strategy*
Mark Boléat
£10.00
1999

Hard Data

1. *The Rowntree Inquiry and 'Trickle Down'*
   Andrew Cooper, Roderick Nye
   £1.00
   1995

2. *Costing the Public Policy Agenda: a week of the* Today *Programme*
   Andrew Cooper
   Unavailable
   1995

3. *Universal Nursery Education & Playgroups*
   Andrew Cooper, Roderick Nye
   £2.00
   1995

4. *Social Security Costs of the Social Chapter*
   Andrew Cooper, Marc Shaw
   £1.00
   1995

5. *What Price a Life?*
   Andrew Cooper, Roderick Nye
   £1.00
   1995

Trident Trust/SMF Contributions to Policy

1. *Welfare to Work: The* America Works *Experience*
   Roderick Nye (Introduction by John Spiers)
   £5.00
   1996

2 *Job Insecurity vs Labour Market Flexibility*
   David Smith (Introduction by John Spiers)
   £5.00
   1997

3. *How Effective is Work Experience?*
   Greg Clark & Katharine Raymond
   £4.00
   1997

Centre for Post-Collectivist Studies Publications

1. *Russia's Stormy Path to Reform*
   Robert Skidelsky (ed.)
   £6.00
   1995

2. *Macroeconomic Stabilisation in Russia: Lessons of Reform, 1992-1995*
Robert Skidelsky, Liam Halligan
£5.00
1996

3. *The End of Order*
Francis Fukuyama
£9.50
1997

4. *From Socialism to Capitalism*
János Kornai
£8.00
1998

5. *The Politics of Economic Reform*
Robert Skidelsky (ed.)
£8.00
1998

6. *The Rise and Fall of the Swedish Model*
Mauricio Rojas
£10.00
1998

7. *Capital Regulation: For and Against*
Robert Skidelsky, Nigel Lawson, John Flemming, Meghnad Desai, Paul Davidson
£5.00
1999

8. *Russia: the 1998 Crisis and Beyond*
Kalin Nikolov
£5.00
1999

9. *Welfare after Communism*
János Kornai
£6.00
1999

Stockholm Network

1. *Millennium Doom: Fallacies About the End of Work*
Mauricio Rojas
£10.00
1999

2. *A European Harmony?*
Kurt Wickman, Philippe Maniere, David Smith, Gunnar Uldall
£6.00
1999